CATCHING DRAGONS

SIMON CHAPMAN

Badger Publishing Limited
Oldmedow Road,
Hardwick Industrial Estate,
King's Lynn PE30 4JJ
Telephone: 01438 791037

www.badgerlearning.co.uk

4 6 8 10 9 7 5

Catching Dragons ISBN 978-1-78147-541-6

Text © Simon Chapman 2014
Complete work © Badger Publishing Limited 2014

All rights reserved. No part of this publication may be reproduced, stored in any form or by any means mechanical, electronic, recording or otherwise without the prior permission of the publisher.

The right of Simon Chapman to be identified as author of this work has been asserted by him in accordance with the Copyright, Designs and Patents Act 1988.

Publisher: Susan Ross
Senior Editor: Danny Pearson
Designer: Fiona Grant

Photos: Cover image: REX/ The Travel Library
Page 4: Juliet Breese
Page 5: Juliet Breese
Page 6: Juliet Breese
Page 8: Juliet Breese
Page 9: Juliet Breese
Page 10: Juliet Breese
Page 11: Juliet Breese
Page 12: Juliet Breese
Page 13: Juliet Breese
Page 14: Juliet Breese
Page 17: Juliet Breese
Page 18: Juliet Breese
Page 19: Juliet Breese
Page 20: Design Pics Inc/REX
Page 22: REX/Monkey Business Images
Page 23: Peter Oxford/Nature Picture/REX
Page 24: Juliet Breese
Page 25: Juliet Breese
Page 26: Juliet Breese
Page 27: Juliet Breese
Page 29: Everett Collection/REX
Page 31: Snap Stills /REX

Attempts to contact all copyright holders have been made.
If any omitted would care to contact Badger Learning, we will be happy to make appropriate arrangements.

CATCHING DRAGONS

Contents

1.	Island of fear	4
2.	Tom-tom drums	9
3.	A brush with death	13
4.	Springing the trap	16
5.	Acid vomit	21
6.	Monster movie	27
	Index	32

Badger LEARNING

1. ISLAND OF FEAR

He was young and rich. She (his wife Katharine) was a beautiful actress. His name was Douglas Burden and he had hired a steam ship called the *SS Dog* to travel to a remote island to look for monsters.

On board the ship there was also a French hunter called Defosse, but this was not a big-game hunting safari. Douglas was on a mission from the Bronx Zoo in New York. His instructions were: "Go and bring us back a dragon!"

The volcanoes of Komodo Island rose up ahead of the ship like a fortress. Just getting to the shore would not be easy.

There was a reef around the island and the water boiled with whirlpool currents.

The captain knew he had to find an open channel if they were to reach the shore. He knew they had gone too far in now to turn around and survive.

A cross-current was taking the ship straight towards the rocks.

"Full steam ahead!" shouted the captain and finally the *SS Dog* pulled past the reef into a calm lagoon.

WOW! facts

For years before its discovery in 1910, there had been rumours of a fearsome beast living on the island of Komodo. Dutch sailors who had sailed their ships nearby said it was a fire breathing dragon, 7 metres long.

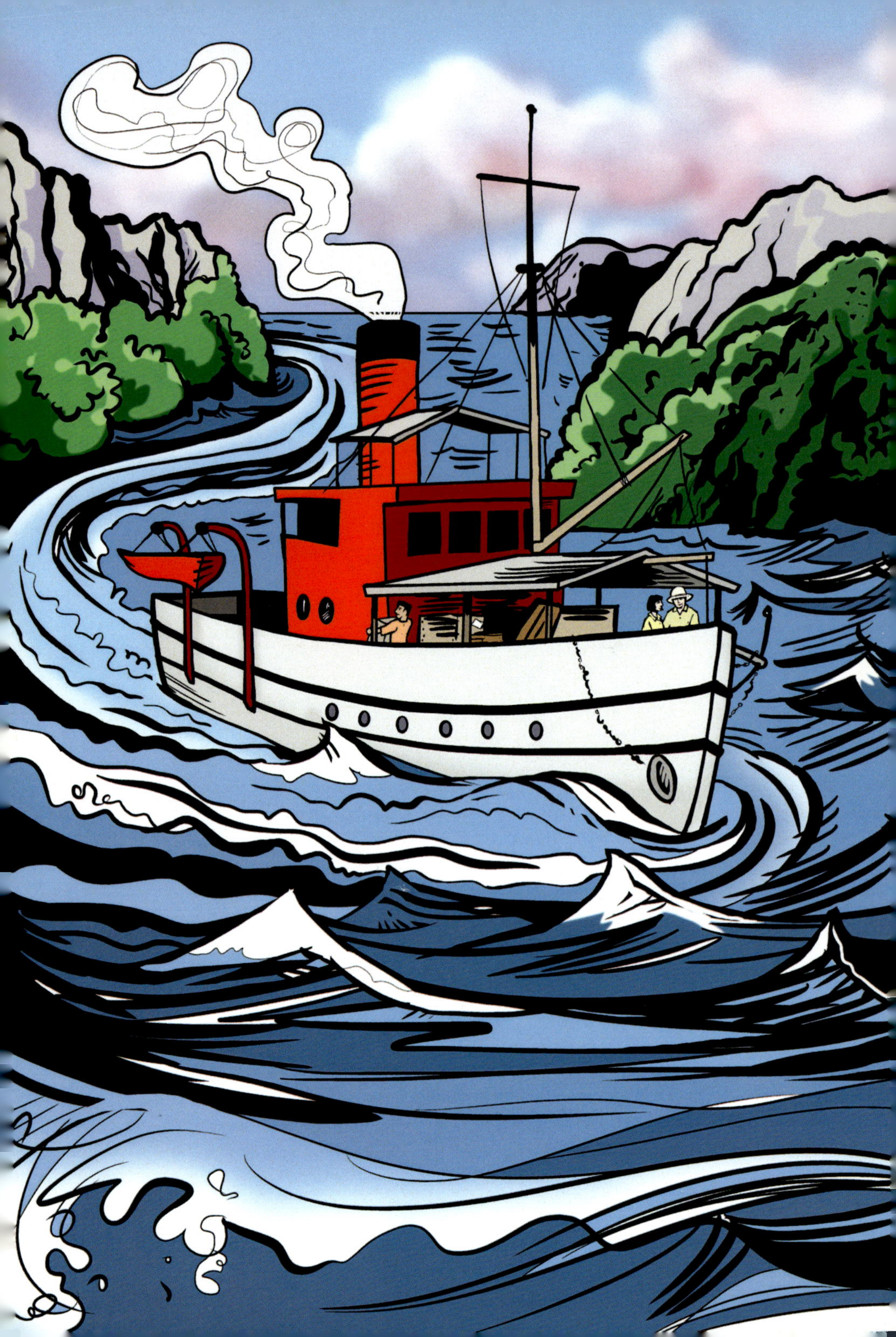

2. TOM-TOM DRUMS

There was a white sandy beach and behind that was a village of bamboo huts. Douglas could see some people there so he started to walk closer. The villagers appeared to be hiding. They looked scared.

"See that graveyard over there," Defosse pointed to a patch of ground covered with rocks. "Those rocks have been put on top to stop something digging up the dead."

"We could make our camp on that ridge near the volcano," he suggested. "It will be safer."

As the group backed off towards the safety of their ship, they heard tom-tom drumming starting up from the village.

"They're signalling," Defosse said. "But I don't know who – or what – to."

WOW! facts

As well as living on the island of Komodo, the dragons also live on several nearby islands, including Flores and Rinca.

Douglas was about to leave when he noticed a strange footprint at the edge of the beach. The track was bigger than his hand and looked like it had been made by a dinosaur.

"Komodo dragon," Defosse said. "That's what we're going to catch."

3. A BRUSH WITH DEATH

It was hot, hard work exploring the volcano's sides.

The jungle was choked with thorny plants. Douglas used a machete to hack his way to a waterfall that splashed over a cliff edge.

He had just moved away from the waterfall and into an open clearing when he sensed something was wrong.

Something was scrabbling up a steep slope, knocking away rocks that came tumbling down behind it.

A lizard – 2.5 metres long, at least – craned its head out from the scrub. Douglas could see the black, beady eye and the grey, scaled skin around its neck.

He could smell the stench of dead meat.

This was what it must be like to come face to face with a dinosaur, he thought.

The beast was still, except for its forked tongue, which flicked in an out, tasting the air for its prey.

Maybe it could taste Douglas's fear. He had to take control of himself and get back under cover.

He had seen a Komodo dragon now, and he thought he knew how to catch it.

WOW! facts

Komodo dragons belong to the monitor lizard family. Water monitor lizards in Sri Lanka have been known to grow to 3 metres long, but they aren't as deadly as Komodo dragons.

4. SPRINGING THE TRAP

The trap was really simple. It had a loop of rope tied to a bent-over tree.

The bait was a dead wild boar. The idea was that a Komodo dragon would go for the meat and get caught in the rope.

The bent tree would then spring up, pulling the lizard into the air. It was a good plan, but things never work out that simply – as Douglas was about to find out.

The problem was there were just too many Komodo dragons around. Most of them were small (only about 1.5 metres long) and these ones were the most inquisitive.

Komodo dragons are cunning. They can sit still for hours, and when they are covered in dust and leaves they look just like dead wood.

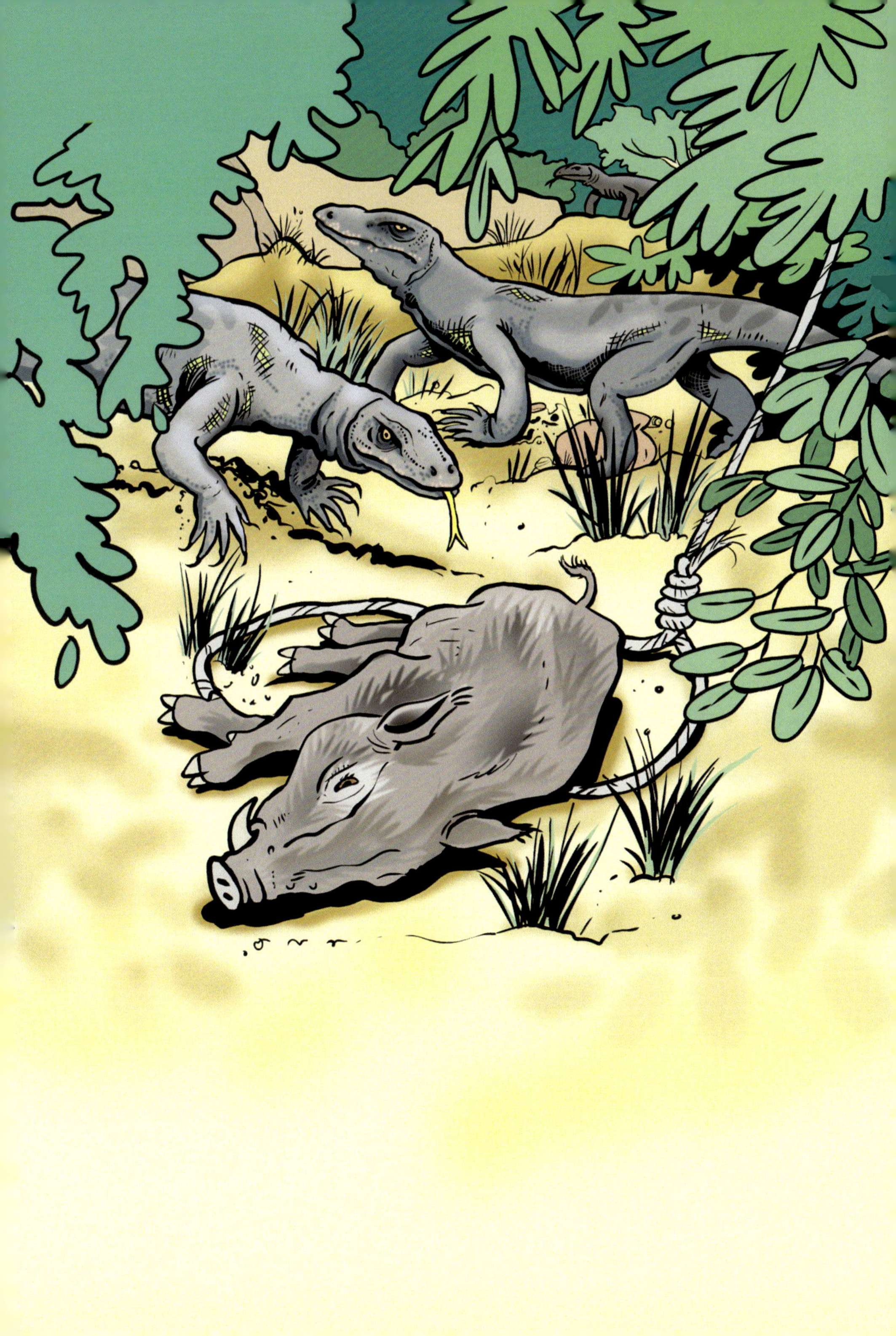

One nearly got Douglas's wife, Katharine.

She had been taking photos of a small dragon that was tugging at the bait. She did not notice the larger one that was creeping up behind her until she suddenly smelled dead meat.

She moved just in time. Seconds later and she would have been bitten, and even a small bite could have killed her.

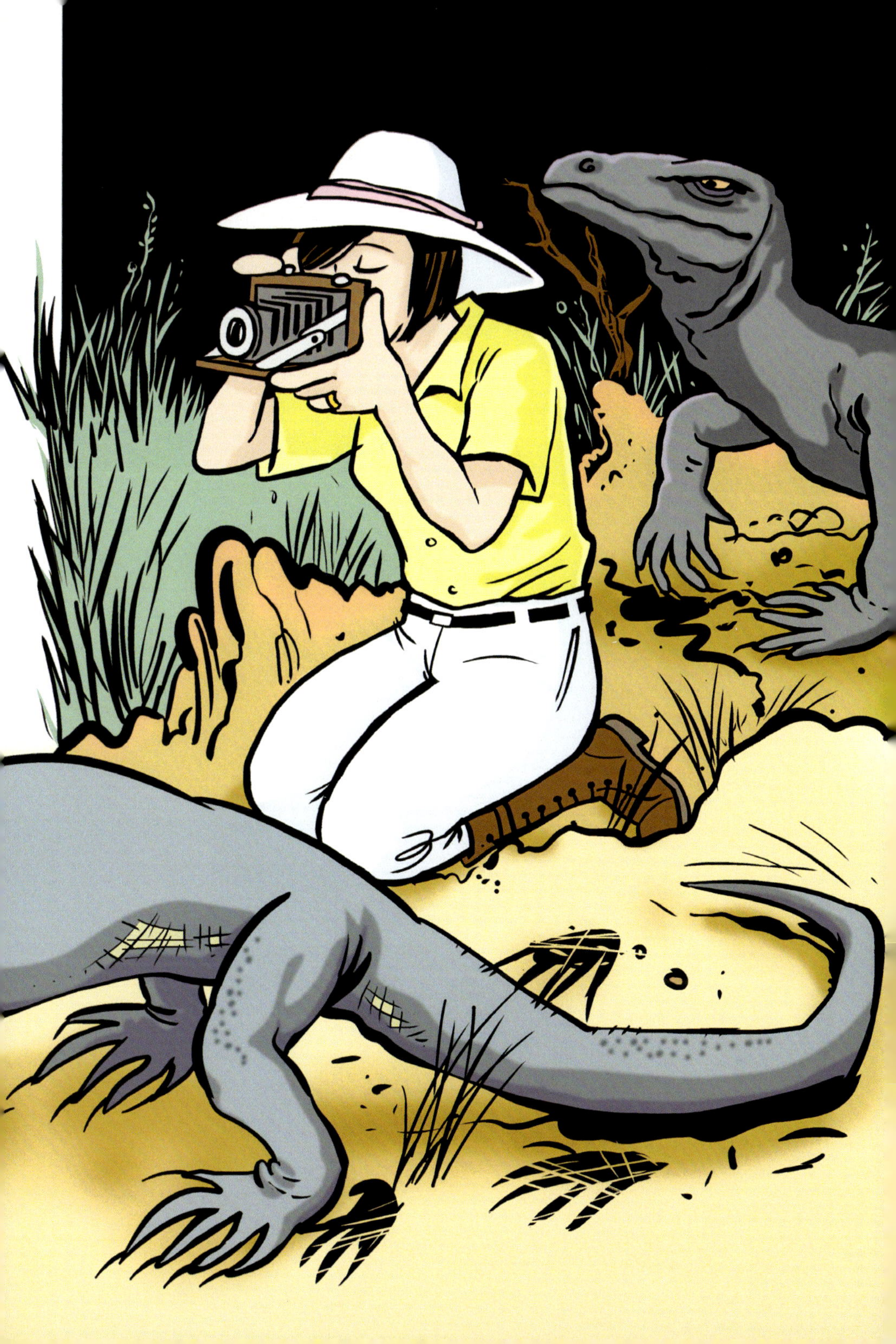

Komodo dragon bites contain venom that weakens their prey. They also have bacteria in their mouths that makes the wounds they inflict go rotten. Komodo dragons have an excellent sense of smell. They 'scent' out their prey and wait while it weakens. Finally, they take it down when it is too sick to fight back.

5. ACID VOMIT

A new plan for catching the dragons was needed. Leaving dead animals out for bait was attracting lizards from all over the island. But how could they trap a big one? Douglas worked out that the trap would have to be set off by a person hiding close-by.

He made a hide of bamboo and woven palm leaves and waited. In the heat of the day he felt like he was in an oven.

The jungle's scorpions and poisonous giant centipedes loved the hot shade. More than once, Douglas had to turn them out of his clothes. Luckily, the noise he made did not scare off the Komodo dragons.

Finally, he saw a huge Komodo dragon, maybe 3.5 metres long, coming his way with its great head swinging from side to side.

This dragon's body was covered with scars. It had fought its way to the top and was 'King of the Jungle' around here.

Now it stood still. It was far too experienced to just go charging into a trap and risk itself. Douglas did not dare move. For half an hour, the big lizard did nothing.

Douglas could feel a centipede wriggling under his shirt but he wasn't going to budge until the monster lizard had its head in the rope loop.

WOW! facts

Some jungle centipedes have venom as deadly as poisonous snakes.

Suddenly, the Komodo dragon made its move. It charged forward, ripping its fangs along the boar's carcass, opening up its insides and spilling out its guts. Douglas pulled.

Thwang! The bent tree sprung up, dragging the reptile clear off the ground. For a moment its teeth were still in the carcass, then that dropped and the beast started thrashing. The tree was creaking. Douglas heard a snapping sound. The dragon's front feet were on the ground and now it was pulling away.

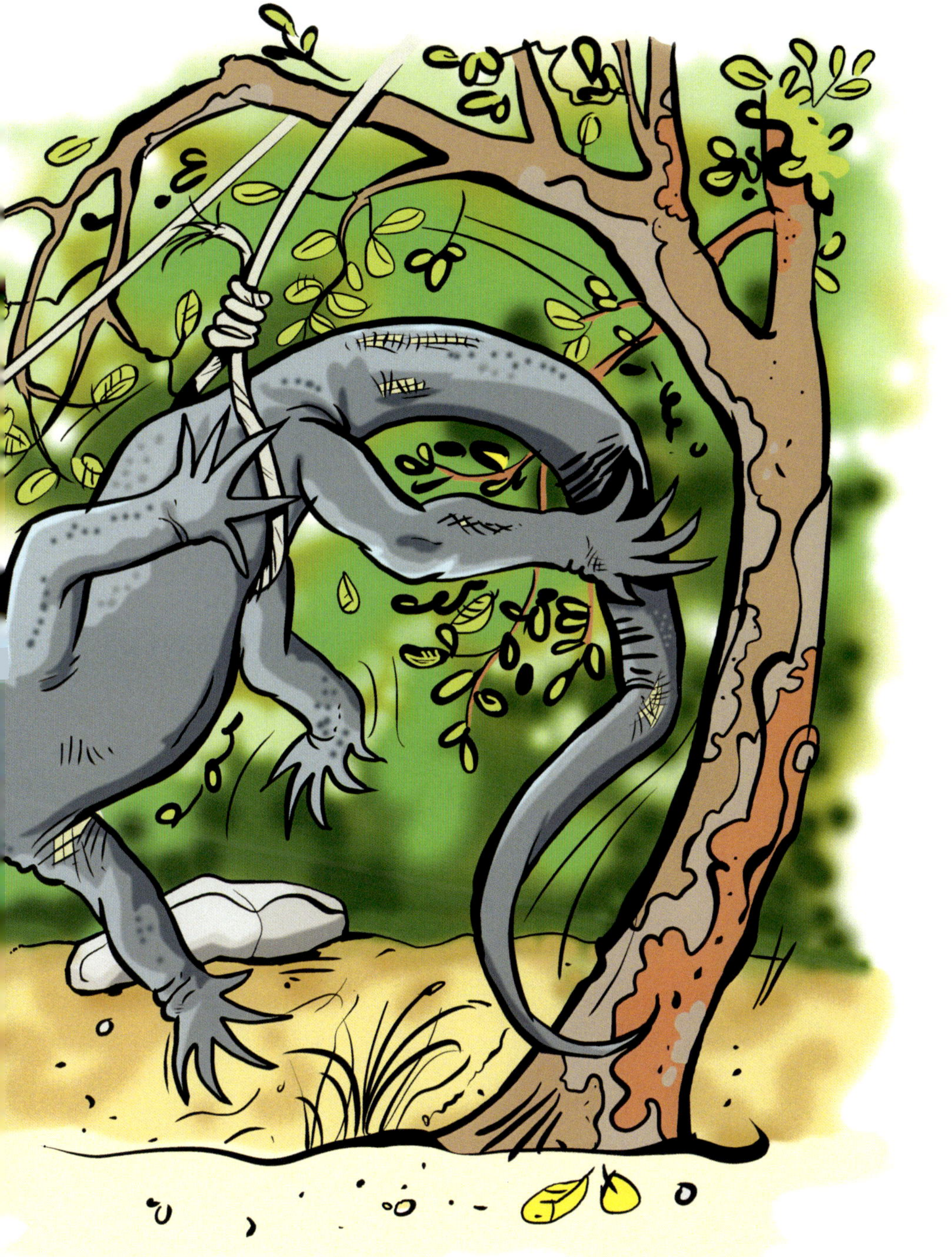

All of a sudden, Defosse was there, lassoing its head. Another man roped its feet but leaped away screaming when the dragon puked acid vomit all over him.

Defosse was still close by, tying more ropes around the lizard until it could no longer move. He and Douglas had caught a Komodo dragon.

They had achieved their mission.

6. MONSTER MOVIE

Douglas had his men carry the tied-up lizard to a cage they had made near the sea shore.

"We'll put it onto the ship tomorrow morning," he said. But Komodo dragons are sly. This one had not been as weak as it had made out.

When Douglas returned the next morning, he found the cage shattered and the dragon gone.

He managed to trap two more, but unfortunately these were smaller.

When he got back to America, Douglas Burden told his story to a Hollywood movie producer.

The filmmaker was taken with the idea of 'beauty and the beast' on a forbidden jungle island and he wanted to make a film. But, he said, Komodo dragons were too small to make the movie work.

"Let's make the monster 12 metres tall," he said. "And let's make it a gorilla."

That movie was released in 1933. It was called *King Kong*.

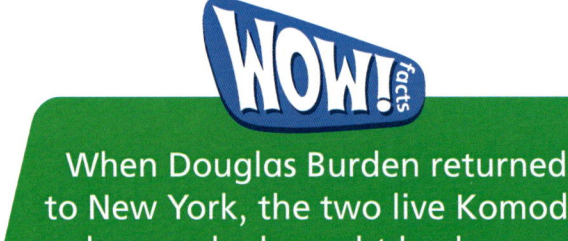

WOW! facts

When Douglas Burden returned to New York, the two live Komodo dragons he brought back were studied by scientists. Afterwards, they went to live in the Bronx Zoo.

KING
KONG
with
FAY WRAY.......
ROBT. ARMSTRONG
BRUCE CABOT...
FROM AN IDEA CONCEIVED BY
EDGAR WALLACE
AND MERIAN C. COOPER
RKO
Radio
PICTURES
DAVID O. SELZNICK
A
COOPER-SCHOEDSACK

King Kong tells the story of a giant gorilla that is caught on a distant jungle island and brought back to New York to be shown off to the public for their amusement.

Kong escapes and, after destroying large parts of New York, he climbs the Empire State Building with a beautiful woman in his hand.

King Kong was first shown in New York and it proved to be a major hit.

There have been many movies featuring King Kong since the 1933 original.

WOW! facts

In the original *King Kong* film the gorilla model used was only 46 centimetres tall and was covered in rabbit fur. In the film he was made to look over 7 metres tall.